# CONNECT 44

## THE 44 LAWS OF HOW TO ATTAIN & MAINTAIN A HEALTHY RELATIONSHIP

## BY ROBERT MINOR

AROMPUBLISHING

# Bibliography

Hale, Mandy. *The Single Woman: Life, Love, and a Dash of Sass.* Thomas Nelson, 2013.

Dickens, Charles. *Our Mutual Friend.* Tauchnitz, 1865.

This book is dedicated to all that I love,
all that I've loved, & to all that loves
me unconditionally.

# TABLE OF CONTENTS

# PREFACE

Growing up, most of us were told that there was someone out there for us and that one day when the time is right, that individual would find us. Though this is something I believe to be very true, there must be effort placed in putting yourself in front of the person of your dreams. The work that needs to be done doesn't start with you just being in front of the right person; it starts with the work, love, and care you put into yourself. Getting the person of your dreams starts with you becoming the person you dream of being. An individual who takes the time and effort to pour into themselves will ultimately pour into their loved ones, specifically their future spouse and children. If you haven't taken the time to envision what you and your ideal family would look like, I'd stress that you'd take the time to do so. Grant it, just because you envision how you want things to be doesn't mean it will pan out exactly how you see it, but it will give you an idea so that you can mentally create a blueprint to go off. Becoming the person you want to become allows you to be the best and most satisfied version of yourself. This version of yourself not only will exude more confidence but also carry an aura that is more appealing to potential mates. Making yourself happy prior to dating a person exclusively is key to attracting the right person, so take the time that you are single to focus on developing the best version of yourself so that you can attract the most ideal mate for you. In this reading, the goal was to give a few guidelines for singles and couples alike to follow to help attain a meaningful relationship and maintain the one they are in. Now the goal of this book is not to give you a blueprint to follow from beginning to end, but everyone who reads should be able to pull a few things out of it to incorporate into their dating life as well as marriage. The family unit is the strongest unit you will ever have in your life, especially if you take the time to choose the right mate, and once you choose the right mate, it will lead to an even stronger unit once marriage and kids are involved. I'd like to encourage all my readers to not only read this book with their own eyes but take what's being said to the heart as well. Internalize it, feel what's being said, and I guarantee you it will be well worth the time you set aside to read it. I wish you all well on your current and future relationship journey and hope that I can be of assistance in helping you attain the partner meant for you.

# LAW 1: YOU ONLY ATTRACT WHAT YOU EXUDE

The law of attraction states that what you set your mind to, you can attract it if you believe. This notion also is true as it pertains to the connection between men and women. Most men and Women will only attract what their energy and mindset allow. Now, most people believe that physical looks are what attracts people to one another, though that's what sparks the initial interest; the real attraction does not start until you are in the presence of an individual. Once conversing with a person and being around them, you begin to exchange energy. At this moment, you begin to feel whether or not a person exudes good vibration or low-level negative vibration. If the individual gives off positive vibrations, the next part of attraction involves the mental connection. Mental stimulation is one of the most important aspects of attraction, if not the most important. Looks may bring you to the table, but where an individual can take you mentally will keep you there. Contrary to what some may believe, helping a person think outside their normal pattern of thought is a turn on to most and is a selling point amongst all individuals. Everyone may not be an intellect, but we all bring some level of expertise and knowledge that can be shared between one another, adding value to someone enhances their understanding, thus heightening the level of attraction among two individuals.

A third element that plays a major part in initial attraction and throughout a relationship is attitude. When you first meet someone, you want to make sure you approach them with a positive disposition. You only have one chance to make a first impression, and your first point of contact can either intrigue an individual leaving them wanting more, or it can leave them displeased, never wanting to be in your presence again. Remember, it's up to you to bring fresh, positive energy to the table. Leaving all old baggage and personal hang-ups in the past, a fresh approach can possibly open an exciting new chapter in your life. It is your call whether you decide to put energy out that attracts or gives off the aura that repels.

# LAW 2: LEAD WITH CHARACTER AND PRINCIPLES

Who are you? What type of foundation do you stand on? These are questions that you should ask yourself before stepping out into the wild world of dating. Before exploring what's out on the dating scene, you must first define who you are as a human being. What is your spiritual stance? Spirituality should be the driving force of all relationships; it is the foundation on which your moral compass and character is built. Entertaining someone who does not have that foundation means you are dealing with someone who does not have values. There are so many instances where a person begins to commit or connect with another individual only to find out that the individual, they've committed to does not live by the same principles as they do. This happens because there was never a serious conversation, giving clarity to the belief system that each person lived by. Instead, the two people dive into a committed relationship, based on superficial reasoning such as looks, status, finance, or sexual attraction, all things that at any time can be taken away from you.

Character is who you are, your makeup, what separates you from others who exist around you. Character is something that leaves an indelible mark in most minds; it's the first thing that people recall when bringing up a person's name. Leading with great character not only separates you from most but also creates an impression that will leave most people intrigued and wanting to explore relationship possibilities. Good character will always be praised and revered, so allowing that to shine through is important when attracting a potential mate.

# LAW 3: YOUR DEGREE SHOULD BE USED TO ATTAIN A CAREER, NOT A RELATIONSHIP!

There was a time when achieving high honors in academia meant a degree to certify your scholastic achievements. It also was a way to create an opportunity in the workforce to receive a good job or great career, but the symbol of a degree has changed drastically. Nowadays, you will often hear men and women claim how educated they are, even boasting of the level of degree they've attained. Don't get me wrong, anyone who has put in the time and effort to complete a successful college journey should be proud of the said achievement. Those of us who have completed this task know that it can be a difficult run, with a lot of ups and downs. Though some potential mates may have this as a must-have on their list of wants when it comes to what they look for in a potential spouse, a college degree should only hold merit in the classroom, not during the dating process. A man that leads with a degree, most likely doesn't have a true go getter mentality or hasn't lived life. Men who understand the world understand that though their achievement in the classroom is important, it's what they plan on doing while out in the world that matters. Men specifically do not put much weight on whether or not their potential partner has a degree or not. The reason is that if he is an alpha male, raised with the principles to provide and protect, he is not concerned with your academic achievement; instead, he is focused on whether you will be a good partner to assist in his life journey.

As far as women are concerned, most tend to show an exuberant amount of pride when speaking of their degree; most even make it a point to let a potential partner know about their achievement countless times. With numerous posts on social media and constant verbal reminders of their accomplishment, most women do not recognize that this achievement is not high on most alphas' list of wants. Don't get me wrong, a person that is an alpha male is pleased if his potential partner does have a college education, but for most, who are true providers and achievers, it is not a deal breaker. As a potential mate, the questions you should ask yourself is, what real-life value can I add to my partner if I were in a relationship? Also, what else do I offer other than a piece of paper, though great to have, is only as valuable as you make it. Last, college achievement aside, what, or who am I without notifying relationship candidates of my degree status.

Remember these questions prior to going out on an intimate date with a relationship prospect, and it may just widen your pool of potentially qualified candidates.

# LAW 4: LOOKS FADE, ATTRACT WITH PERSONALITY.

Growing up, one of my favorite movies was "Shallow Hal" starring Jack Black. Hal, played by Black, was a superficial male who, with the advice of his father, only dated physically attractive women. Hal was advised to only recognize women's inner beauty after going to a convention and meeting self-help expert Tony Robbins (Yes, thee Tony Robbins). From that moment on, Hal visually could only see beauty in women that were not considered physically attractive to most. As human beings, it is natural for us to be physically attracted to one another before any other attraction occurs. I mean, you see a person way before you speak with them, so obviously, their looks will be the first thing that gravitates you towards the individual, but you should not allow this alone to be a determinant on rather or not you decide to entertain a possible relationship with a person of interest.

We all hope that we can look good for a long period of time, but the fact is, most people will not. Many things may play a factor in the decline of a person's looks, including genetics, old age, weight gain, and countless other natural changes. There are also those who are victims of accidents or medical issues that can change one's appearance for a long period of time, if not forever. Connecting with an individual's personality and becoming Intune with a person's spirit should be your focus. Yes, you should be physically attracted to the individual, but as my mechanic would say, "it looks good on the outside, but what's under the hood". It's cliché to say, but it truly is what's on the inside that counts. A person who does not possess a good spirit, ambition, drive, loyalty, among many other honorable qualities, cannot truly be a solid addition to your life. With that said, allow vanity to be near the bottom of your list of needs.

# LAW 5: ALWAYS STAY F.L.Y (FIRST LOVE YOURSELF)

One of the greatest loves a person can have is the love for self. Not in a narcissistic, egotistical way, but in a way that builds long-lasting confidence and self-appreciation. Love for self, overrides love for anyone else because without self-admiration there is no way you can reciprocate that feeling to another human being. Failed relationships & courtships can have many factors, but one of the lease spoken about is the lack of self-love by one or both individuals. Self-admiration starts at an early age; your parents or guardian begin to show their love for you on a regular basis, which in turn, begins to build you up inside and out. That love and self-worth built inside of you by your loved ones begins to show on the outside and can be seen and felt by those who choose to see and receive it. This is how self-love begins, and this love allows those who are blessed with it to share it with those around them, especially a potential mate.

The opposite side of self-love tends to happen in the opposite sequence; a person did not grow up surrounded by love; they were not taught self-worth, thus making it almost impossible for them to receive love or give love to others. If you are an individual who does not have self-love, don't worry, it can be resolved. Rather, you decide to speak with those in your family who you felt should have been responsible for teaching you self-worth, or you seek professional assistance from a licensed therapist; closing that old wound is a necessary action prior to you sharing & receiving love from a companion.

# LAW 6: LEARN FROM THOSE WHO INFLUENCE YOU (LEARN FROM OTHERS SUCCESS AND MISTAKES)

They say the best teachers are those with experience in what they are teaching; this statement is one hundred percent true. For those who fall under the category of single and ready to mingle, you should first take the time to look at your surroundings. In terms of what a relationship should look like, most individuals first point of reference is mom and dad. Mom and dad are normally the first people that show you an example of how relationships work under any and every circumstance. As most people grow up, they are normally around their parents on a regular basis; this allows a child to witness all things good and slightly, if not totally dysfunctional. For those who witnessed a healthy relationship, you were blessed to see positive displays of affection, such as kissing, hugging, holding hands, even joking and laughter. These visuals helped to shape your understanding of how love is expressed and how affection is shown. Now, we are all human beings, and as human beings, we have differences;

with that being said, even in a healthy relationship, human beings have their ups and downs, and these ups and downs will sometimes be seen by a child as well. Disagreements among adults often occur due to lack of understanding, miscommunication, different upbringing, or even financial woes, just to name a few. These types of interactions are normal for adults to have with one another, as long as it doesn't' happen often or in an intense manner. Everyone wasn't raised by their biological parents; some were raised by their grandparents or aunts and uncles. There are children that are raised by their adopted parents or come from single-parent households, but regardless of who raises them, if love is expressed in a positive way, then children will pick up the positive habits being displayed in the household. As the children grow into adulthood, the ways in which they saw loved expression will be mimicked in their own marriage and eventually passed down to their children. Now, though many of these learned behaviors are adopted at an early age, even as an adult, it is important to observe the functionality of the relationships around you. Not only should you continue to watch your family members, but also observe your friends, your mentors, even your spiritual leaders' relationships, using them as positive as well as negative examples as you explore the dating scene.

The same way an individual can pick up good relationship habits by observing healthy practices, a person can also pick up unhealthy behavior by being surrounded by toxic couples. Being a witness to constant arguing can make a person feel as though you can only convey a message by screaming back and forth with your partner. A person that was a witness to physical abuse can be traumatized in a completely different way. Seeing a loved one or friend being abused often can mentally scar a person, especially one that has not grown up or ever been around positive examples of love. We all should take the time to see what surrounds us, noticing what others are doing can assist in how you shape your current or future relationship. Observe, take mental notes, then apply what you deem as healthy to your own romantic relationship.

# LAW 7: MAKE SERVITUDE A HABIT.

Charles Dickens once said, "No person is useless in this world who lightens the burdens of others." Relationships are about give and take, sometimes you must be the individual that gives cooperation and servitude to your spouse and sometimes, you should be the one who receives. When I say servitude, I don't mean a person should act as a maid; however, a couple should take the time to care for one another. Becoming someone's peace of mind is important on so many levels. Creating a stress-free environment for your partner may include domestic tasks, such as cooking, cleaning, and organizing. It may be making sure that you are allowing your partner to concentrate on the task that would allow them to better themselves, thus bettering the living situation for the both of you. Taking care of your spouse means checking in on their mental health, making sure they are in a good head space so that they can conquer this traitorous world head-on. It is vital that you check your partner's health, preparing meals for one another that are healthy and balanced, giving your partner the nourishment they need to maintain a good bill of health. Serving your partner should not be a gut-wrenching task that feels like a dead-end job. However, it should be a way of life that should be implemented regularly to create a nurturing environment.

# LAW 8: A GREAT FRIEND MAKES A GREAT SPOUSE.

I was once told as a little boy that when I decide to get married, I should make sure I marry my best friend because no one's going to know you better than your best friend. I will carry those words forever, and I will pass them down to others because I see that to be true. Before ever becoming someone's lover, you should first become their most trusted friend. If you plan on occupying a person's time for life, it's pertinent that you become fully in tune with that individual. True friends have each other's best interests no matter what the circumstance. If there's honesty and loyalty among the two individuals, the strength of their bond will be virtually unbreakable. Another thing you should pay attention to is how good a friend or a person is or isn't. Most people may not realize it but take your friends or family, for instance; if you were to evaluate most of the ones who are in constantly failed relationships, I guarantee most of them probably aren't necessarily great friends. Of course, there are other factors that can play a part in a person not being able to maintain a healthy relationship, such as upbringing and past trauma, but for the most part, you will notice that those individuals are not the greatest of friends. Those individuals normally are selfish, lack empathy, are not attentive, undependable, and refuse to evolve in the friendship department. So, the next time you are around friends and family that are always dating and single, monitor how they are as friends, and I guarantee you will see the reason why they have never been able to maintain a strong romantic relationship. With that said, contrary to what some people believe about the dynamics of relationships, there should be no difference between the friendship you maintain with your peers and the one you have with your significant other. Where things differ is when it pertains to the feeling of love. The love you have for a friend will be based on time, experiences with one another, as well as the commonality and connection you share with each other. Though those forms of connections are the same as those you will have with your significant other, there will also be an intimate connection that binds two partners together even closer. Dating your best friend will allow you to have the best results when it comes to a healthy, long-lasting relationship, so keep your eyes open; your soulmate may be the person you share laughs with on a regular basis.

# LAW 9: EVERYTHING IS NOT FOR EVERYONE; STAY IN YOUR LANE.

The old saying goes, "everything isn't for everybody", this could not be more correct. When choosing a mate, you must be realistic with who suits you best. Though we all should have some level of expectations, those expectations should never be too low and never be too high. Leaning in one direction or another will leave you full of disappointment, with someone lesser than what you need, or alone. The best way to understand where your expectations should be starts with a simple question, what do I bring to the table. One of, if not the most avoided questions when it comes to self-evaluation. Recognizing your value in terms of the relationship market will allow you to either upgrade yourself so that you can find a better partner; it will also give you a clear picture of where your expectations should be. Case and point. If you are an individual who does not work out, does not read research often, is financially illiterate, then you cannot expect to get a partner with a six-pack, well-read, with a large bank account, and a good career. Now don't get me wrong, I'm not one to think anyone should think that they are better than anyone else but know your worth. An adult living with their parents that is not saving for a house, working a mediocre job, should not expect to find a partner that has their own place, working for a fortune 500 company: it's unrealistic. Are there stories where someone catches lighting in a bottle, and a person connects with someone that has it all while they have nothing, of course, but that is a rare instance, and when searching for a mate that is not what you want to rely on. Shoot for the sky but understand if you haven't worked or been blessed in a way that would have you grab a star, no worries, there is someone out there for you; just make sure it is for you!

# LAW 10: TREAT THE RELATIONSHIP MARKET LIKE THE STOCK MARKET.

The true value of a company's stock is called its intrinsic value in the stock market. Intrinsic value is the true dollar amount of a company's worth; this includes tangible and intangible factors. This concept is easy to grasp for most who invest in the market, so what if we used this same concept when choosing a mate? What if you chose a mate based on the actual value that the individual brings to those who he or she encounters? Falling in love with a person is one thing; falling in love with a person that adds actual value to your life and those around them is another. An individual who adds value helps those around them grow, rather or not it's direct or indirect. When dating someone who adds value, your value and worth spike as well, thus like the growth in your stock portfolio and the value of your overall net assets.

Another way people could relate to the stock market to find the right mate is by understanding market trends. Market trends when it pertains to the stock market are ways to gauge rather or not the market is trending up or down; how can you relate this to the dating market? Social media is a good way to know what dating trends are happening. Are more couples being formed because of dating apps? Are clubs and lounges the places to be to meet that significant other? How about courtship, what are people doing to keep the interest of a potential mate? These are all things that can be seen on social media, thus giving you a decent understanding of what the dating market looks like.

# LAW 11: COOPERATION IS THE DRIVER OF A BALANCED RELATIONSHIP.

To get what cooperation means regarding a relationship, you must understand why it is necessary. To make things function properly in a relationship, there must be understanding, followed by an agreement. The agreement should consist of each person's role in the relationship at that current time. For example, suppose one person brings in the bulk of the income. In that case, there should be an agreement that, that individual should be allowed to focus as much as possible, without disturbance on whatever that individual does to generate their income.

Cooperation cannot be met by itself; it must correlate with assurance from the man, assuring the woman that the household's financial needs will be taken care of. There also should be reassurance of protection, the man's job is to provide and protect. If those basic needs are met, the woman should give full cooperation, allowing the man to do their job at a prominent level, creating a better living environment for the family.

# LAW 12: DEFINE YOUR OWN RELATIONSHIP GOALS; STOP MIMICKING SOCIAL MEDIA.

Relationship goals, you see this tag line plastered all over the social media stratosphere. Rather you are surfing through Twitter or scrolling on your Instagram feed, memes of celebrity couples, social media influencers, and couples matching everything flood your timeline. Tags such as "Relationship goals," "This could be us", and countless others are burnt into your subconscious. Vacation photos on sunny islands and elaborate dinner date still shots, further remind you that your dating life is lackluster, or is it? The greatest part about social media is we all can connect with one another no matter which part of the globe we are in. On the downside, false facades are created, leading to false perceptions, which ultimately misleads those who may or may not know how to separate social media from reality.

A photo can show you a lot of things, but it cannot give you a realistic view of a person's relationship with their significant other. I can personally tell you about scenarios where I've seen couples argue just minutes after taking a photo that everyone labeled as goals. All relationships should have a list of goals, short-term and long, that should be attempted to be met over time. These goals may include a house, children, businesses, among other things, but these goals should not be influenced by a still shot of couples which you do not know personally or do not know what goes on after the camera flashes. Make it a point to be your own goals, focus on what you and your partner need to accomplish, and never become envious of social media highlight reels.

# LAW 13: ADVICE FROM SINGLE PEOPLE WILL MAKE YOU ONE OF THEM.

Sometimes the best advice to give is no advice, especially when you are not an expert in the topic on which you are being advised on. Friends and family tend to want to give advice to help those they love to get through or over a situation that may be negatively affecting your life. One of the subjects that tend to get the most feedback is relationships and how to manage them. When taking relationship advice from another individual, be it family or not, be mindful of who it is you are taking advice from. You need to ask yourself a few questions prior to taking advice from anyone giving you tips on what to do in a romantic situation. First off, what is their relationship status? Are they happily married, are they single, have they been in a long-term relationship for a while? Someone who is not or does not have prior experience in being in a long-term relationship or marriage should not be your go-to when it comes to attaining and maintaining a long-lasting relationship. A professional sports team would be reluctant to take advice on how to win from a coach whose record is 0-500, so why would you take advice from an individual who has several failed relationship attempts? A person who has never displayed an example of a successful, meaningful relationship should not, I repeat, should not be giving advice to someone on the market for a significant other. Not to say that because a person is single, they should not give advice because there could be several reasons why an individual is currently single, such as divorce, death of a spouse, infidelity, just to name a few. The people who should not give out relationship advice are those who are toxic when it comes to romantic relationships. Those who have only been in short-term relationships, those who are socialite wana bees that cannot settle themselves long enough to be with one person, those who do not know how to communicate with a potential mate, thus always leaving prospects disinterested. These are just a few examples of those you may want to avoid taking relationship advice from. If looking to gain true insight and knowledge of how to maintain a relationship, look to a person that has been married for some time. Not only can they give you the ups, but the downs as well, allowing you to see what it takes to truly be a real partner. You can also look at those who have been in long-term relationships, at least five years or better, but for one reason or another did not work out, but they came out better afterwards. Those people can give you a true visual of growth because not only did they try to make a relationship work, but they also grew into an even better candidate for a long-term partner through their own personal growth. Once again, be mindful of who you take advice from because it could be the difference between success and failure.

# LAW 14: IF THE RELATIONSHIP IS NOT DEFINED, IT DOESN'T EXIST.

Nowadays there are relationships that exist that are known as "situationship". A "situationship" is a relationship that is undefined; there are no titles, there is no commitment; thus, there truly is no relationship. These types of relationships should be reserved for high school and college-aged students; you know, people who should make good use of their youth to explore different personalities and relationships so that they know what they like, dislike, and would love to explore later down the line. This "situationship" style relationship should not be entertained by anyone past the age of twenty-three. As an adult, you should aim to do adult things, and be involved in adult-style relationships, be it romantic, personal, or business. The most valuable thing we have as human beings is time, so wasting time with childish interactions and relationships should be avoided at all costs. Allowing your good years to be squandered away on a person who does not and will not ever like or truly value you or your time is a recipe for lonely years to come.

# LAW 15: YOUR CELEBRITY CRUSH DOES NOT WANT YOU; DREAMS ONLY COME TO THOSE IN TUNE WITH REALITY.

We all grow up having a celebrity crush; sometimes multiples; it is a normal thing to experience. We constantly see these people on television, and on the big screen, we look at them with admiration and are amazed by all the wonderful things they project through the screen. We fall in love with these celebrities, so deep in love that we believe that we would be desirable to them. Some people even go as far as to use their celebrity crush as the bar they set to choose a mate, thereby creating unrealistic expectations for themselves and those they choose to date. The fact is, the work ethic, the sacrifice, and fearlessness that it took for that person to get to where they are, you most likely don't have. Now, this does not just apply to celebrities but highly valued individuals in general, meaning those who put it all on the line and take care of themselves physically and mentally, achieving what most consider impossible. To attract those types of people you admire, you must display confidence that is only found in a small percentage of individuals. You must embody an insatiable appetite for success and achievement not only for yourself but for your partner. You must stay physically fit, making fitness and health a lifestyle, creating, and maintaining a visual that will not only attract that level of high value but keeps that high-value person interested in years to follow. Allowing celebrities to be the criteria in which you date is not only immature but ridiculous because the truth is you are buying into a person who plays a character, and they may not be all that you perceive them to be in real life.

# LAW 16: WHATEVER ATTRACTED YOUR PARTNER SHOULD NEVER BE ABANDONED.

As I touched on earlier, initial attraction is normally in the form of the physical. We notice their looks since we cannot see a person's brain or achievements at first glance. First, noticing an individual's shape and build, we can immediately tell one of three things, either that person is a gym rat, has good genes, or does not watch what they put in their body. In some cases, weight gain, specifically for women, can be due to past pregnancy medical conditions; among other issues, those circumstances should be met with understanding. Suppose you are a single person that consistently goes to the gym, and maintains a healthy body weight, once in a relationship; this is a practice that should be kept up barring injury, illness, or pregnancy. Due to sheer neglect and laziness, letting yourself go should not be accepted or tolerated by a significant other. Partners in a romantic relationship must realize that once you physically let yourself go, you are visually not the same person that your partner met. It shows that you do not care to be physically appealing to your significant other, displaying a level of comfort in the relationship that lacks self-pride.

Skin care is also important to maintain before and after you are in a relationship. Make it a point to cleanse your face, get rid of pimples, scars and blemishes as best you can. Healthy skin gives you a glow that your spouse or future partner will never forget. Regularly taking care of your hair and nails is also necessary. To maintain strong nails, we all should be taking vitamins and other natural supplements such as zinc. Make it a point to often visit your local salon or barber to keep your hair groomed and ready for any occasion. When you look good, you feel good, and when you feel good, you give off great energy that will attract and keep a mate attracted to you. Last but certainly not least, take care of those teeth. Two things that catch people's attention instantly are an infectious smile and nice clear eyes. Attend your annual sixth-month checkups so that you can get your teeth properly, deeply cleaned, and scaled. A healthy smile is unforgettable, so don't forget to protect it. Self-care is the best care, so make sure you care for yourself so that someone will make the same effort to properly care for you.

Now I know I spoke a lot about the visual aspect of keeping your mate attracted to you, but what about the mental aspect?

Some tend to become overly comfortable in a relationship, to the point of becoming lackadaisical. That drive and ambition that attracted the person you are with should never be put off to the side. If you came into your relationship wanting more out of life, speaking about big goals and wants and desires, that should never be abandoned due to comfort. Just know that some men and women will take you for who you are no matter what, but is that necessarily a good thing? In some cases, yes, no one should be left out in the cold because of unforeseen circumstances; that is not a reason to lose interest in a person. However, no man or woman should accept or be willing to be accepted by someone who allows them to not be the best version of themselves. That leads to regret down the line and shows that you truly do not care about that person reaching their maximum potential. Whatever it was they did to get you, never allow anyone to stop doing what it is they did to keep you.

# LAW 17: REVEAL, THEN HEAL.

One of the hardest things for most human beings to do is get past the issues and trauma of their past. Now in terms of the past, this could mean past romantic relationships; this could mean past long-term friendships which ended traumatically. This could also go even further back to childhood; in any case, these types of problems, if not remedied, can become toxic and problematic to any and every future relationship. A hurt person cannot be of value in a relationship because they are not all mentally or emotionally there. An incomplete person will not be able to connect with a better half and create a whole relationship until they decide to face their past hurt and/or demons that have never been dealt with.

The first thing one should do is begin to get themselves centered spiritually. This does not necessarily mean you have to belong to a traditional religion or religious group, but you do need to connect with a higher power, the universe, and what is most forgotten nature. Becoming emersed in spirituality, gaining a level of awakening that allows you to become knowledgeable of self and in tune with your surroundings; this is the beginning of the self-healing process. Next, it's time to reveal; the revealing process involves extensive communication, which means communicating or conversing with a trusted friend, family member, spiritual leader, or a licensed therapist. I would personally suggest doing all three because the more you are able to reveal your hurt and pain, the sooner you will be able to begin the full-on healing process.

Remember that all trauma and pain are not created equal, so the extent of the help a person may need would be relative to their issues. For example, someone dealing with death, specifically sudden death or murder, may need more counseling than someone who suffered the expected loss of a loved one. Not to say that loss isn't loss, but a person who was not mentally, emotionally, or financially prepared for a loved one's passing, may be in more of a shock or dealing with mental anguish. As talked about In Law 6, what you witnessed in your life as a child can cause issues, especially if it was a negative experience. Witnessing such things as physical and mental abuse of a parent or relative could leave a psychological scar that you may not realize exists until you get older and are introduced to the same style of abuse in your own personal relationship. For some, it may cause them to seek that type of relationship because that is all they are accustomed to seeing, and for others, it may not allow them to be emotionally available in a relationship. Infidelity is another traumatic experience that can deter people from relationships or not allow that person to trust while in a relationship. Rather you witnessed infidelity in your own home, or you personally dealt with it in past relationships, this could cause you to feel unassured in any relationship, no matter how well your new partner treats you. The overall path to healing is revealing yourself, your pain, your hurt, and your truth; this is what needs to take place for total recovery to begin and new relationships to blossom.

# LAW 18: A PERSON WILL ONLY TREAT YOU HOW YOU TREAT YOURSELF.

How do you view yourself? This is a question that every person on the planet needs to ponder when self-evaluating oneself. How you look at, feel, and treat yourself is how someone will feel comfortable treating you. With social media and camera phones everywhere, people tend to forget that there is a watchful eye on everyone, nearly around the clock. Since we never know who's watching, whether it's on social media platforms or in real life, we must be more cognitive of what we say and do in public. When trying to attract a partner, the worst thing you can do is get caught in the wrong light on social media. In today's age, direct messaging is 50% of people's first point of contact; displaying yourself on social media in an unappealing, uncouth manner repeatedly could shy the person of your dreams away from ever reaching out to you.

Though we may not always like it, we are always marketing ourselves to people who may want to buy into us. No different from if you were auditioning for a part in a movie or interviewing for a job, you must present yourself in a way that would attract someone to want to buy into you. People will only see what you present to the public, and how you view yourself; keep this in mind the next time you find yourself posting or allowing others to post you in an unflattering light.

# LAW 19: STOP GIVING AWAY YOUR GOOD YEARS TO THE WRONG CANDIDATE.

Time waits for no one, and neither does a good candidate for a spouse. We only have so much time in a day; why waste it entertaining someone with whom there is no potential future? Grant it, to understand what you like and dislike you must go out and meet different people, & occasionally date a few. Getting a feel for what turns you on and what deters you from potential mates is a natural part of the dating and selection process but understand that you do not have an infinite amount of time to waste, so be mindful of this while taking a swim in the dating pool.

When getting into a relationship, it is important to first know why I am in this relationship? Does this relationship add value to my life? Are we compatible in all the ways necessary to grow as a strong unit? If any of the answers to these questions are no, you may need to evaluate why you are involved with the person you are with. Unfortunately, there are countless people in the world that involve themselves in long-term relationships that end up becoming a huge waste of time.

There are several reasons why this happens, but it is mostly due to one of three things. One, people tend to waste time in relationships because they are dangerously comfortable with the person that they are with. Now, what do I mean by dangerously comfortable? This means, in a relationship, two people could be together for such a long period of time that even with no growth or lack of hope of a real future, the two will continue to endure one another out of fear of being lonely and the avoidance of anxiety brought on by the unknown dating world. The second reason most people waste their good years in meaningless relationships is due to not understanding what the dynamic of a fulfilling relationship really is. We all have our idea of what a romantic relationship is, but most are clueless about what it should be. Once again, this is an issue caused by a lack of good examples being present in a person's life and never having a solid visual representation of what a stable, loving relationship looks like. The third and final reason most people involve themselves in hopeless relationships is that most do not know how to value themselves, thus not understanding their self-worth. Look at it from an angle of applying for a new job, after being interviewed by an employer, one of the last two statements made is the salary in which they are willing to offer a future employee. Normally, most people just accept the position and salary without evaluating the offer and countering with a salary that better reflects your worth, often leaving thousands on the table due to not knowing your value and being afraid of asking for what you want. The same is true when it comes to relationships; most never recognize or reevaluate their value, thus accepting and staying with a partner that does not match or equal their current level of growth. The danger of this is if an individual stays with an unsuitable partner too long, just like the vehicle sitting in your driveway, your value begins to depreciate. I am not stating if you overstay your welcome in a dead relationship that you will be forever single; of course not, that is an absurd thought because you will find someone once you are ready to place yourself back on the market. However, what you will be able to attract after overstaying a relationship will be less than what you would have been able to get beforehand. There can be many factors to this truth; for one, you may have built a family with the person that you wasted years with. This does not apply to all relationships where children were conceived, but it does, however, affect those who brought children into the world while in a dead-end relationship. Another factor is time wasted equals age gained. You may look young, but you do not age backwards; what was once for you is most likely now off the dating market. While giving your precious years away to an unworthy partner, you age yourself out of a broad dating pool shrinking it down to whatever's left over. It is possible that you find a diamond in the rough, but most good catches are off the market between ages 24 to 33. With all that said, make it a point not to waste time on lifeless relationships because what is meant for you will not remain available forever.

# LAW 20: THOSE WHO CHOOSE NOT TO DISCONNECT WILL NEVER MAKE A CONNECTION.

It is no secret that personality is one of the main keys to attraction; your personal story also draws people into who you are and what you are about. Unfortunately, with overutilization of social media, it has created a sea of socially inept individuals. Over usage has not only weakened face-to-face communication but also has put a strain on verbal conversation. When's the last time you've seen people go out to dinner without thumbing through their phone half the evening? Lack of attentiveness has become a common thing currently; human beings have literally become disconnected from one another and increasingly more connected with an inanimate object.

Why does this matter? "I pay my cell phone bill; why can't I do what I want with my phone"? You are right, it is your phone, and you can do whatever you want with it, but here's the problem with that. According to Linda Andrews of physcologytoday.com, overuse of cell phones can cause mental fatigue, disengaged parenting, and, yes, damaged romantic relationships. You cannot expect to connect with anyone on a human level if you constantly seek that dopamine shot given by likes and social media engagement. A few ways to remedy this problem, one chooses a few times out the day to disconnect from social media and your cell phone in general. Stop relying on social media to be your first source of news and information. Learn to look up information about current events on your own. Have more face-to-face encounters with those you are dating, less texting, less direct messaging, and more dinner dates without phones, more walks, more dates in nature and on the beach; this will boost your desire for human interaction. You control you and your relationship, don't allow technology to be the side person (device) that ends that.

# LAW 21: IF YOU DO NOT INTRIGUE WHEN SEARCHING FOR A MATE, YOU WILL NOT SUCCEED.

When having a one-on-one conversation with someone, can you hold the attention of the individual longer than 5 minutes? Do people constantly want to hear you speak due to your expertise, your experience, or how you eloquently express yourself while discussing a subject matter? Are people constantly asking you to elaborate more on a certain topic that you discuss while giving you their undivided attention? When in conversation, do you constantly hear statements like, "that is amazing", "I've never met anyone that has done that before", and "I would love to go there" or "do that"? If so, you are on the right path; you are a part of the minority that knows how to captivate another individual's attention just through basic conversation.

Keeping the attention of a potential mate during one-on-one interaction is a necessity and a skill set. It shows that you, as an individual, have exceptional social skills and a way of connecting with others on a personal, emotional, & Intellectual level. As I talked about before in the previous chapter, most do not know how to stay connected enough with human beings due to their over connection to social media. This lack of connection has caused damaging effects for over a decade now, and with Generation Z becoming even more emersed in social media interaction and validation, it does not seem as though things will become any better anytime soon, especially with things such as the Metaverse on the horizon.

Though this issue seems to be one that will be problematic, here is the advantage for those who choose to practice balance. For one, those who still exercise in-person social interaction will have an immense advantage over those who choose to connect primarily from social media platforms. You will stand out among a crowd full of social media-controlled human robots, utilizing eye contact, verbal communication, and emotional connection to make a true connection with the proper mate. Another advantage is that those who can truly master the art of human connection and social media interaction will become an expert. You would truly be the person that people can go to for relationship advice in today's times if you so choose to be that individual. Regardless of how much things change, one thing is certain, humans are emotional beings who need to be heard, seen, comforted, and most of all loved; this fact will remain true as long as we exist here on earth.

# LAW 22: ONLY CHAMPIONS WIN RINGS.

This chapter is geared directly toward women in a relationship. Every woman believes they deserve an engagement ring at some point in their relationship but may not understand what it takes to get that prize. Just like sports, those who get rings earn them with dedication, effort, and hard work. When a man decides to choose who to take as a life partner, many factors come into play. First and foremost, spiritual connection has to be the first and most important factor as it is the foundation of any solid relationship. What you are rooted in spiritually is what drives you and will drive your relationship and marriage until lifes end. With this factor, there is no room for compromise; if the two parties are not aligned spiritually, then the relationship will never last. Men also look for nurturing and attentive women; this quality is becoming scarce in today's times, but it is very telling in regard to how a woman will care for children when & if they choose to build a family. Earning a ring is not solely based on love; in fact, that is only 25% percent of the reasoning.

Another 25% is based on the value that you add to the person that you are dealing with. Just being present is not enough; how do you help your partner or potential mate grow? Does the person tend to gain when they are around you or take losses? These are things that need to be monitored by all parties and to evaluate whether or not holy matrimony should even be a thought. The next 25%, which I am biased about, is peace of mind and serenity. I find this one to be most important because, for the man, the breadwinner, the protector, to perform their life task effectively, there needs to be peace spread throughout the home environment by his woman. What this means is creating solitude in parts of the home so that the male can think, create, plot, and plan on how to take the world head on, on a regular basis. Creating a hostile environment full of arguing, noise, and unnecessary tension, not only creates an unsuitable environment for building and creating but stunts the overall growth of a prosperous relationship. The last 25% to round it out is based on overall goals. True winners have goals, and their goals are aggressively attacked on a regular basis. Having goals that align with the man is important when you desire to spend the rest of your life with that person. Your goals should be discussed on a weekly basis; I would suggest every few days; this is necessary for understanding where you see yourself heading as a couple. Goals should be the first discussion conducted on the first date. What each party wants out of life and how they plan to get it should be known from the very beginning. True winners take the necessary steps to earn the ultimate prize because in this world, everything is earned; nothing is given.

# LAW 23: THE VISUALLY UNAPPEALING SHOULD MAINTAIN A GORGEOUS PERSONALITY.

G rowing up, I was told that beauty is only skin deep, but ugly is to the core. This is a saying that I've carried with me through the years and has proven to be true. Rather, you are considered physically beautiful or not attractive at all, how your inner beauty projects to the general public leaves a lasting impression on most people. People tend to always recall a sweet and polite person; they never forget the person who was witty and charming. On the flip side, people tend to never forget those who present themselves in a rude, obnoxious way. Harboring ugly feelings while displaying undesirable personality traits is a deterrent for sane, nontoxic individuals.

So why does looks play a part in all this? Though attitude plays a large part in how people perceive you, looks determine what people may be willing to tolerate from you. For instance, a more physically attractive person may have a little more leeway when it comes to projecting a less than tolerable attitude. The reason this takes place is because a person dealing with the attractive individual will allow that person's visual appeal to take precedence over their attitude. A less attractive person would not be offered the same level of elbow room when it comes to how their attitude is presented. The less physically attractive individual needs to lead with personality because they do not have the luxury of distracting potential mates with their beauty. Granted, beauty is in the eye of the beholder; but there are universal beauty standards that most would agree with. We all can agree that a woman like Jennifer Lopez or a Man like the "Roc" are physically attractive; I'd bank on at least 90% of people would agree with that consensus. Though some are attracted or settle for those less physically unappealing, there is no doubt that those people also agree with universal beauty standards. With all that being said, if you are not the most attractive person in the world, so what! No worries, just make a conscious effort to exude an exuberant amount of confidence & joy, because truth be told, most looks fade at the end anyway, but a vibrant, intoxicating personality will always stay intact.

# LAW 24: ENVISION WHAT YOU WANT OUT OF A RELATIONSHIP & FAMILY, THE SAME WAY YOU DO YOUR CAREER ASPIRATIONS.

While planning what we can of our future career-wise, we tend to have no issue with setting lofty goals. We will purchase whiteboards and markers and write down our goals step by step. People will throw vision board parties, buying and grabbing every magazine they can get so that they can cut them up and express their wants and desires through photos. Some of the more ambitious individuals will even find a friend, coworker, or mentor, to be their accountability partner. This is customary practice when plotting for a prosperous year. This common practice without doubt, should be incorporated in everyone's planning process when it comes to laying out their future; the same method should also be applied when putting together what you would like to have in a mate.

Most tend not to take their search for a suitable companion seriously; they either do not know what they want or don't understand what suits them best. Some people even live in a fantasy bubble and want something that is not for them. For example, if you are an individual who is a social butterfly, you should aim to find an individual who either is just as social, if not more than you or a person who may stay out of the way but does not mind how gregarious you are. Compatibility is what keeps a relationship alive; connecting the yen to your yang will not only keep things pleasant but will also add to the strength of the relationship.

I recently watched an old interview with the legendary Kobe Bryant, and he was asked how he knew his wife was the one. And the character traits that he mentioned stood out to me; he said that she had great qualities that would make her a good mother, she also had a competitive nature like his. Characteristics are incredibly important when choosing a mate; we tend to forget who we are when choosing the right person. Knowing who you are is extremely important when you are making yourself available to a potential mate. If you are in the dark about who you are & who aspire to be as an individual, how can you find someone who is evenly yoked with you? Tap into your likes and dislikes, your wants and desires, your peace, as well as your strength. Become what you want to attract, foresee what you would hope your life would be while in a relationship, this way you will know what is for you and what was not meant to ever be in your presents.

# LAW 25: UNDERSTAND LOVE LANGUAGES.

As adults, one thing we tend to neglect to understand when involving ourselves in a relationship is how we enjoy receiving love from our companion. Understanding your partners' love language is important when looking to gain a deeper connection with that person as the relationship matures. Growth in a relationship only takes place when you are truly in tune with how the person you are with wants and needs to be loved. There are five well-known love languages, and most, if not all people can identify with at least one of. One is positive affirmation; when your partner encourages what you are doing, giving you praise, cheering you on like your biggest fan as you tackle your goals, how does that make you feel? If this type of expression from your partner brings a euphoric feeling over you, then this may be your love language. The second love language is acts of service. When your partner performs acts of kindness for the community or for you, relieving you of burdens or stress, is this something that tingles your spine? If so, then acts of service may be your love language of choice. Are you a lover of gifts? I mean, everyone loves gifts, but not everyone feels a closer connection to their partner after receiving them. If you feel a stronger connection to your partner after receiving a thoughtful, heartfelt gift, then receiving presents from your partner may be the way to your heart. The fourth love language and most common is quality time. Though this seems simple enough, for a substantial number of people, especially successful ones, this can be the most difficult love language to carry out regularly. Though most want to take the time out to go on vacation, go out to eat, or just sit on the couch and watch a movie, at times, it can be difficult depending on schedule and obligations. That being said, understanding that time is the most valuable thing we have, we all should make it a point to carve out time to spend with the ones that we love; this alone can strengthen the bond between two people. The last love language but certainly not least, is number five, the language of physical touch. The handholding, kissing, hugging, cuddling and even subtle touches are all ways that you can show your mate that they are loved. Number five would seem like common knowledge, yet a good portion of individuals neglect to express themselves in this manner towards people who find joy in receiving love this way. For a bonus, let me throw in a sixth love language, and that's food, yes food. Taking your significant other out to eat at a nice restaurant, experiencing fine cuisine, or just fulfilling your hunger needs, is one of the most thoughtful love languages there is. It is even more so when either the man or woman makes a home-cooked meal for their partner or even the whole family. Shopping for food, carefully preparing the food, cooking the food, and at the end of it, all providing nourishment for your partner or the whole family is one of the most expressive forms of true love and care, even more so when the gesture is performed without asking that silly question "are you hungry."

If we want to build healthy, long-lasting relationships, we must work at it. We must tell our partner what makes us feel loved, and we need to show our partner love in the way that they want to receive it. That is how we can use love languages to improve the quality of our relationships.

# LAW 26: START EARLY DON'T WASTE TIME "FAKE LIVING".

The most valuable thing in the world we have is time; we can't buy it, we can't trade for it, and we certainly can't go backwards in it. Therefore, it is important to spend your time making meaningful choices, enjoying every second while adding value and memories during every minute. Because our time here on earth is unknown, the importance of not wasting it is as important as how you spend it. There are people from all walks of life who believe that they have all the time in the world and that they can choose to get in a relationship whenever they see fit. These individuals will spend pivotal years participating in unnecessary partying and engaging in useless activities while squandering away their good dating years with individuals they clearly have no long-term future with. Years that could have been spent connecting with a person whom they could have grown and built with, are occupied by those just looking to have nothing more than a good time. Of course, you must date & converse with others to see what you like, what you dislike, what turns you on, and of course, what turns you completely off. You should also use your period of being unattached to explore the world, travel, become in tune with other cultures, figure out who you are as an individual because this all contributes to the natural maturation process, but like any period in your life, it all has an expiration date. Be mindful of where you are in life and where you would like to be. Be heedful; it is important not to frivol away time participating in activities that will shed a bad light on who you are or take away from the time that you should be putting into a relationship that will ultimately lead to building a family. We all believe that we are living because we have breath in our body, when in fact, you can be the walking dead, wasting time, depleting yourself of energy that you will never get back while congregating with family and friends that do not have or want what you claim you are looking for out of a relationship and a family. Your future is dependent on how you live your life; make sure you spend your time living with a purpose and not existing in a falsified lifestyle.

# LAW 27: DO NOT BECOME THE OLD MF IN THE CLUB.

There is a time to work and a time to play, but unfortunately, some choose to overindulge in the latter. Having a good time with friends is a wonderful experience; it can even be a much-needed stress reliever but be aware that time waits for no one, and we are all on the clock. Partying in your early to mid-twenties is normal; it's the time when you are fully introduced to the world, getting to meet new people throughout the area you reside, learning yourself inside and out. However, frequently partying in your late twenties well into your thirties, now that is another story. During that time in your life, you should be on the verge of settling down, building wealth, connecting to a partner, and creating the foundation for your own family structure. For those who continue to party into their thirties, not only are you wasting time, as we touched on with law 26, but you are now beginning to compete with younger adults who are in the same position you were in 10 years prior, and because of their age & potential, may look to be a better option. Know when it is time to walk away from the nightlife, be cognizant when the new generation begins to enter the party scene. You need to focus on becoming the example of a person in a healthy relationship at a certain point in your life and not the adversary of the generation preceding you. Time creeps up like a thief in the night, don't be the person who gets caught up because they do not want to relinquish the night life.

# LAW 28: LOOKS FADE, INTELECT AND MORAL VALUES STAY SEXY FOREVER.

As we begin to get older, we transform, our faces begin to look a bit different, our body's ability to perform at a high-level change, our feelings about certain aspects of life and the world even take on a newfound outlook. Though looks are an important factor, it should not be the only factor when choosing a mate, and in most cases, it should not be a deciding factor. The two things that do not change, and will not change, is an individual's intellectual ability and the moral foundation of which the person has been raised. Baring mental illness, or unforeseen circumstances, the knowledge that a person attains over time is one of, if not the most valuable asset that an individual possesses. The lessons that you can learn from a person who has taken the time to become well-read is something that only a few can attest to. According to statista.com, the average person spends 0.11 of an hour reading per day, which is equal to seven minutes per day. 74 percent of Americans, according to statista.com, have said to read only one book per year. These statistics are mind-boggling but could be used to the advantage of those not only looking to become more knowledgeable about life, spirituality, and the world around them, but it can also become a great selling point when looking for a mate. The knowledge we possess has value on all levels; among our families, it allows us to educate and feed them mentally, propelling them to a higher level of understanding, which will become beneficial to the greater good of the household. From a spiritual aspect, it assists immensely in the overall building of the foundation of the family. Finally, within a relationship, the knowledge you attain and the values you build allow it to grow and flourish, ultimately leading to a sturdy foundation and wisdom that will help the parties involved maintain a long-lasting well-rounded relationship. Hanging your entire relationship decision-making on the balance of vanity can be a costly mistake; not only will you begin to shrink the pool of potential mates, but you will also dilute the quality of individuals you deem as fit companions. Looks have a great deal of importance, but without any substance, you are just dating the exterior of a person.

# LAW 29: LOVE IS THE AGREEMENT OF THE HEART; MARRIAGE IS BUSINESS CONTRACT.

So, what is marriage? Most people view marriage as a holy covenant under which two people commit to one another under the eyes of God. Though this is part of the definition of marriage, it is not the complete meaning of the union where two become one. Merriam-Webster.com defines marriage as "the state of being united as spouses in a consensual and contractual relationship recognized by law." Marriage.com states that the concept of marriage is an agreement between two individuals that both are willing to accept for the duration of their natural life. The one thing that stood out to me most when going over several definitions of marriage was that the term love was never brought up, not even once. Now I will be honest, reviewing several readings, I was shocked that I could not find a reference to love at least once in any of the readings, but though shocked, I was not blown away by this finding. Ever since we were children relationships & the union of marriage have been depicted as this fairy tale of the knight and shining armor magically appearing and sweeping the woman off her feet. The two would fall madly in love, then one evening he would give her the most memorable proposal, a year later, the couple would have this big, beautiful wedding, then go off to live happily ever after. Of course, this chain of events can take place, and do, but what isn't discussed is the business aspect of the union of marriage. Marriage, specifically in the United States and varying countries, is an agreement between two individuals to spend the rest of their lives together. This agreement is made official not through the celebration of the union, which is marriage, but through a legally binding contract. Contracts such as community property, ante nuptial, and even age-old marriage contracts are just a few that are used to bind the two individuals together while protecting their assets in the case of the contractual agreement being broken by one or both parties. Though love has always been one of the selling points of marriage, it has nothing to do with the actual legal union; in fact, love is an agreement all on its own. The agreement of love is the agreement made between the heart, mind, body, and spirit of two individuals who would like to put their selfishness to the side and become one in the future. Love has no written contract or legally binding documentation. Love is not something that the state or any other part of government has a say in. Love is not just a four-letter word but a way of being, feeling, and expressing oneself to the person your heart truly lies with. Though society tends to intertwine the two, Love and Marriage are not the same, and understanding the difference is key to the overall union's success.

# LAW 30: THE "IF THIS WERE TO HAPPEN" CONVERSATION MUST HAPPEN TO PRESERVE THE RELATIONSHIP. PLANNING FOR SEPARATION WILL KEEP THINGS TOGETHER.

I spoke earlier about how important communication is in a relationship; it can shape if, and how long a relationship will last. One conversation I added to my communication skills is a hypothetical "if this were to happen" discussion. Now I will be honest with you; this discussion was nothing I read about or stumbled upon; it was literally a moment where I wanted to make things clear; if something were to happen, these are the steps that should be taken. Unknown to me, this discussion worked in a way that I could not have imagined; not only did it get things out in the open without the professional assistance of a therapist, but it brought clarity to how my significant other and I looked at pitfalls that could take place.

So, what is the "if this were to happen" discussion? The "if this were to happen" discussion is a detailed hypothetical discussion that a couple engages in, breaking down what-if scenarios and pre-planning how to manage each scenario. The importance of this type of conversation is to begin to think logically about what could be looked at as a traumatic, life-altering situation. Take for example, most do not like to think about the passing of their significant other, and rightfully so, but the importance of knowing how to handle what needs to be done after the fact is extremely necessary. In the event of an untimely passing, there are many t's that need to be crossed, and I's that need to be dotted. The first thing that needs to be taken care of is the funeral arrangements and burial plans and how these things will be funded. During the hypothetical discussion, you will begin to discuss details such as life insurance, living will, as well as building trust to protect your estate and assets. Conversing about things of this nature allows you to think with a clear mind and plan accordingly, preparing legal documentation that will protect the lost loved one's assets so that there are no financial discrepancies when that time comes. Now the discussion about if a spouse was to pass is uncomfortable but not uncommon, but what about if your spouse wanted a divorce or your significant other came across another person better suited for them? Yes, you read this correctly; though this is not the most comfortable or typical conversation to have, it should be considered. Life happens, and nobody is perfect or immune to a potential break in a relationship, this is where the "if this were to happen" conversation is masterful. Through this style of communication, you and your partner will allow yourselves to be vulnerable and think through potential scenarios that would change the shape of the relationship. Take for instance, say you and your partner had been dating for a year or so, and as they begin to upgrade themselves in society, they come across another individual that is better suited for them in the long run, a person more evenly yoked if you will, your reaction based solely off raw emotion may be volatile, but what if you had, had the talk? We are human beings, and we all have emotions, but what if this scenario was discussed months or years prior to? You'd be placing yourself in a better headspace to think through your reaction in a more logical manner. But the discussion does not just work for the spouse who may feel hurt; it also allows the other partner to learn how to present unsettling news in a respectable way, eliminating deceit and argumentative style communication. Some relationships have children involved; the "if this were to happen" conversation allows couples to intelligently discuss how they would present and communicate their situation to their kids; it also gives the parents a chance to think through what would be best for the children in that hypothetical circumstance. These types of talks are tough, without question, but allowing yourself to think through worst-case scenario situations allows you to prepare yourself in an effective way, creating less damage and a more optimum outcome.

# WHAT IF QUESTIONAIRE

In this couple's exercise, create three scenarios that could potentially lead to the relationship being dissolved if not handled correctly. Begin with what needs to be done to rectify the issue or what should be done to salvage the relationship if possible. Are there children involved, if so, how can you create a comfortable space where the children can thrive & not be affected by issues between the parents? Are there finances involved, if so, worst case scenario, the relationship ends, who takes care of what? End your hypothetical scenario by Asking yourself, does love outweigh the issue at hand?

| Questionnaire Details | |
|---|---|
| Scenario 1 | |
| Scenario 2 | |

| What If Questions | |
|---|---|
| Question #1 | |
| Notes | |

| | |
|---|---|
| Question #2 | |
| Notes | |

| Question #3 | |
|---|---|
| Notes | |

**Enter Additional Notes.**

# (FOR WOMEN) LAW 31: HAVING A VAGINA IS NOT THE ONLY CRITERIA FOR BEING A WIFE.

Though not written in stone, there are universal standards that exist for being a Husband & Wife. We may not want to admit or follow these standards due to the newly found standards created by some members of the female population, but what it takes to be a wife has existed way before the birth of millennials and most of generation x. With the emergence of the feminism movement back in 1848 with the Seneca falls convention, the reemergence between 1963 & 1976, and the third wave in 2016, how women have viewed their role in the home has changed drastically. The mention of basic survival skills such as cooking and cleaning has turned into a violation of women's rights, and to a select few, the conversation is looked at as archaic, but is it? Should it be an issue for a man to expect his future wife or current spouse to perform simple household duties, duties that no matter what, needs to be taken care of? Should a man not want to feel love in the form of a home-cooked meal & nourishment? If a man wears the weight of the family's monetary responsibility, should he not expect at times to get catered to? Before going on your journey of searching for a mate, be sure to self-evaluate, figure out whether you are fully qualified to be the female in that man's life to help propel him to the next level of his life's journey. It is easy to say what you want as an individual, but what you need to be as a partner tends to be overlooked. Another question that should be touched upon is, do you understand what it takes to be with a man that is an overachiever in life? There are some women who claim to want a wealthy overachieving man, but do you know what is required of you as a partner to attract and maintain that man? A woman who wants to be with an over achiever must expect to stay physically fit, well maintained on a regular basis, and keep a versatile yet classy wardrobe because one thing that is attached to a high-achieving man is appearances amongst the upper echelon of the world, so your presentation is ultimately a reflection of him. Throwing cocktail and dinner parties is also a part of being with a high-achieving man; this is all a part of the social aspect of assisting in propelling your partner to the next plateau of his career and life. How is your conversation, are you interesting? We have talked about this in a previous chapter, but most women & men tend to think they are more interesting than they truly are & in some cases, they are but have never expressed themselves fully to anyone to really show that side of themselves. A high-achieving man wants to be mentally stimulated no different than a high-achieving woman, so make sure that when you are dealing with or putting yourself on the market to attract a man of this caliber, you must know that they want someone intriguing with captivating conversation and falling short will leave him uninterested. The last question you should ponder is, if this man that I want, wants children, am I truly a nurture? Are you willing and capable of raising a high-achieving child? A high-achieving man wants to create and raise high-achieving offspring and will not settle for a partner who is fine with mediocrity. Being the person who can fulfill a man's needs, no matter what tax bracket or stage of life he is in, is a challenge meant for the right spouse. Understand the wants and needs of the type of man you hope to get, and become that partner that they need, and watch how you attract the ideal spouse that you want.

# (FOR MEN) LAW 32: YOUR WOMAN WANTS A MAN, NOT A GROWN CHILD.

As human beings, we all have our issues. Some issues stem from past family and social trauma; some come from old relationships, which impacted our lives negatively? Some issues even tend to come from what one has witnessed among our own parents and siblings. Regardless of how the trauma came about, it is important to seek professional counseling to touch on those issues hindering your mental progression. With men, we tend to shy away from taking care of our mental wellness, bottling up our problems, hiding and drowning them with work, hobbies, and silence. This erroneous way of bottling up everything until the man explodes is archaic and one of the leading causes of toxicity and immature habits within a romantic relationship. Women who date or marry men want a man that is a true Alpha in every sense of the word. A protector, provider, basically an overall leader, but being a leader takes mental stability and a level of maturity that will help the relationship grow to its full potential.

So how does all this adversely affect the woman in the relationship? It's simple; a woman can't grow in a relationship if she constantly has to babysit the emotions of her male partner. Now, the same could be said for a man in the same situation, though most men will take the approach of either they'll deal with the emotional baggage or cut the woman off completely. A woman, on the other hand, will stick it out with her partner, especially if she truly loves and cares for the man she is with. No female deserves half a man in a relationship, especially not one who is giving her all. Before any man entertains the thought of being in a committed relationship, he must first ask himself, am I mentally, emotionally, spiritually stable enough to become a suitable partner for a female companion. The next thing a man should ask himself is, have I truly worked on me. Taking the time to work on yourself is something that I will touch on in more depth in the final chapter because it is extremely critical and important to know who you are and who you want to become so that you can be everything you need to be to the person you are in a relationship with. The last thing men need to do that most men do not do is talking issues out with other men. There is no better way to better yourself as a man than to discuss things with other battle-tested male figures. The insight you can attain from a male who has been in your shoes is valuable & can further your overall progression.

# LAW 33: CONSISTENCY IS KEY.

How one goes about choosing a significant other can be based on many things, loyalty, trust, work ethic, strong values, among many other qualities, but what is the root of all these qualities? As if the title of this chapter was not a dead giveaway, it is consistency. Consistency is performing the same way at various times, meaning no matter what is taking place, you bring the same energy, work ethic, level of loyalty, etc. So, what does consistency mean regarding a relationship? The generic short answer is, everything, but let's break down what consistency looks like when dating. When dating someone, one of the most telling qualities of a person is how consistent they are with their action towards you. How a person treats you in public, how a person treats you when you are among family and friends, and how they care for you regularly are just a few things that will assess your partners' consistency. Consistency in a relationship means dependability; a man & especially a woman, wants to know that they can count on their partner in any situation. No matter how tough times are or how wonderful things are going, your partner wants to know that you will be there in the same compacity no matter what. Currently, most would say it is tough to find someone who is consistent with their behavior and how they go about treating someone they are dating, and there are many factors to this, but the two main reasons, in my opinion, are people becoming overly comfortable & social media. Now you may ask, how does social media factor into a person staying consistent with their partner? The reason is this, social media causes distraction, and distraction throws us off focus, which is the most principal factor in being a consistent person. It takes focus to be able to constantly do something at an elevated level, in the same manner each time. For example, if you are dating a person and you always compliment them on how they look, you've set a standard or a pattern of telling your significant other that they look good. If for some reason, you go a month or months without complimenting that person, it may cause friction. Now, of course, if you have personal issues going on in your life, that is understandable & something I hope would be understood & recognized by your significant other, but what if there is no good reason? What if the only reason you did not pay attention to your significant other was due to the fact that you stopped focusing on them? What if you stopped focusing on their wants and needs for that week and lost sight of their likes and dislikes? Now, forgetting to compliment someone regularly may seem like a small thing, but that may be a big part of the relationship for some. That may be how that particular couple bonds with one another, and if that form of bonding is all of a sudden being compromised due to the fact that the boyfriend or girlfriend lost sight of what the other expects from them, then it can make the other partner begin to question the consistency of the person with whom they are in a relationship with. Consistency in a relationship is about dependability; it is continuing to do the things that you've done previously to attain and maintain a healthy relationship. Never letting up or getting overly comfortable with doing what you do to make a person feel special, cared for, and safe makes that individual feel appreciated and gives them a sense of stability, knowing that you will be there when needed. So once again, how does social media play a role in hurting the consistency within a relationship? Though social media is good for a lot of things, it is also a major distraction. The constant posting of the opposite sex flaunting everything from their bodies to their possessions can make even the strongest or most attentive person lose focus and get lost in a false reality. For a man, it can make him underappreciate his woman, making him feel that he is missing out on all these beautiful "fun, available women", when in fact, he has or is working on what they are campaigning for on a daily basis, via social media post. The same can be said for women, scrolling through social media watching men post their material possessions, making her feel as though maybe she can do better or should be receiving more. Even though both parties may not be phased by going through their social media app from time to time, if constantly on social media, you eventually start to adopt the mentality created by over-exposure to the imagery you see.

Showing consistency in a marriage is even more important because you've already set the foundation and probably have shown a great deal of consistency which got you to the place of matrimony, to begin with. The biggest issue in most marriages when it pertains to lack of consistency is that one or both parties become overly comfortable and begin to let their foot off the gas of the driving force that led to them becoming one. Just because you are married does not mean you stop treating your spouse the same way that you promised you would, you took a vow, and your job is to honor it. Continuing to be who you have always been does not only make your spouse feel comfortable and secure, but also brings a sense of familiarity to the aged relationship. Whatever you did to place yourself in a successful relationship should not be abandoned due to becoming overly comfortable or lazy. Stay the course and remain the person that your significant other took an interest in and grew to love in the very beginning.

# LAW 34: TIK FOR TAC IS FOR KIDS; RETALIATION DOES NOT BALANCE OUT A RELATIONSHIP.

A strong relationship is built off honor and trust, compromising either of those things will cause a great deal of conflict among the two parties involved in the relationship. In today's time, infidelity has become a norm, so much so that it is almost expected at some point. But even with this expectation, there is still a feeling of deception that is felt by the party that has been betrayed. Now, a wise person would either leave the negative situation or forgive and hopefully grow from it, but nowadays, that is not the case. People tend to do unto others as they had done to them, trying to find a sense of relief by making the other party feel the same pain that they felt when they decided to betray them. Now, there are many things that are wrong with this approach; for one, you can't mask hurt by inflicting pain yourself, especially not emotional pain. Emotional pain hurts, more than physical, because it is burnt into your mind, and that feeling is something that you can always recall. When someone hurts you and it affects you emotionally, it can leave a scar that is tough to get rid of. Trying to heal that pain by participating in the same act that your partner participated in shows immaturity, and it is not productive. Trying to inflict emotional pain on an untrustworthy partner can also create unhealthy habits in future relationships. You will feel that the way to get over any form of betrayal is to retaliate against your partner, when in fact, that is the very opposite of what you should be doing. Instead of taking a negative act and creating a negative response, use that hurt to create a new. Learn from what took place in your life and grow from it, learn what you do not' like and make sure you do not ignore the signs during your next relationship.

# LAW 35: TAKE ADVANTAGE OF ALONE.

Author Mandy Hale writes, "There are some places in life where you can only go alone. Embrace the beauty of your solo journey", and no truer words could have been written. Your solo journey will be the second most important journey in your life, only second to your spiritual journey. This is the time when you will find out exactly who you are and build up the foundation of what you hope to become. During your time alone, every individual should take advantage of minimal to no distractions, the time where you choose to practice discipline and focus. Just you and your thoughts will be when you begin to plot which direction you hope to go in, in your life. At this time in your life, selfishness is warranted, only thinking about yourself, your needs, and your goals; this selfishness will lead to your future selflessness that will be displayed and shared with your future family. Most do not take advantage of alone, mainly because alone can become prosaic. Being alone can become a playground for wild thoughts and impulsive decision-making for those who do not have the drive to push forward through life on their own. Standing by yourself through your maturation process is a key step in making you whole as an individual, and there is no way you can complete another human being, relationship-wise, without fully knowing who you are and what you are aiming to become.

# LAW 36: GUARD YOUR HEALTHY RELATIONSHIP WITH SILENCE.

There's a saying that I created after noticing how relationships are portrayed and displayed in today's time, it goes, "The one who shows their relationship often to the world will soon be displaying their single status". So, what does this mean exactly? In this day and age, people need validation for everything they do in life, rather it's how they look, what they eat, where they vacation, and even who they date. People are always looking for some form of approval from those they know and even strangers they don't. This approval can come in the form of a like on social media, a thumbs up on YouTube, or even traditional verbal acknowledgement and praise. This type of validation should not be necessary when it comes to who you select as a significant other, especially if that validation does not come from close family and friends who want the best for you. You should not be concerned with what those in the social media world think of your relationship or how it is going. Letting one or two people have an inside look at the affairs of your relationship can ruin it, so how do you think letting thousands or even millions inside your business will affect your love life. Now, this not only applies to new relationships but also to those who have been together for a while and even married. The social media universe, when it pertains to relationships, is unkind. There are plenty of individuals who sit in misery, some alone, some in worthless relationships, on their phones watching every move you make, just looking for any kind of dirt they can find. As soon as one mistake is made and seen by the public, they are ready to do anything to try and destroy what you have. The best way to protect a happy, healthy relationship is to enjoy it in silence. No need to post your partner as he or she is driving; that is your moment to relax with your loved one. Nobody needs to see you two lying in bed with one another; that time is intimate. No one even has to see photos of the two of you on vacation; hell, you can take separate pics, no one even needs to know who's taking the pictures; hell, somebody is taking those mother F#*!ers, and it's not the business of any of the onlookers wondering. Your love life is your business, and what you choose to share is up to your discretion. Just be mindful that though there will be tons of people who praise what you have going, there is even more who are rooting for it to fail, so play it smart and control what they see & do not feed in to what they "hear".

# LAW 37: ALWAYS AVOID A MARRIAGE LESS, OR CHILDLESS, COMMUNITY. YOUR TRIBE DETERMINES YOUR CHILD'S FUTURE.

When most begin to seek a significant other, it's all about finding that right person, getting to know them, getting in tune with their personality, gaining an understanding of who they are. During this process, this is the time to really vet who you are dealing with; this is also the time to investigate the individual's family dynamics and the group of friends they associate with. Now, we can all agree that it is important to investigate a person's family situation, especially someone you see a future with. Mental illness, drug, and alcohol abuse, relationship dynamics, are just a few of the things that you should be looking into while getting to know someone who may be around for the long haul. One thing that tends to get overlooked is the structure of the family. Now, what exactly do I mean in terms of structure? What is the marriage to single ratio in the family? Now some may ask why this is important, but as I wrote in earlier chapters, what an individual grows up around and sees on a regular basis will be things that they practice. Now, just because someone grows up around a family where most aren't married does not mean they will not choose to get married; in some cases, people gravitate towards what they've never seen personally or lived around out of the aspiration to attain it. Unfortunately most individuals who come from families who have little to no married individuals tend not to get married because of the lack of exposure to the loving sanctity of the union. This obviously is important to know when dating an individual, especially one that you may see a future with, cause although that person may check off a lot of boxes, the fact that that person has never had examples of long-lasting relationships may cause them to be apprehensive when it comes to moving things forward in the relationship, if not avoiding marriage & and building a family all together.

Another dynamic that people tend to overlook when it comes to vetting a potential mate is the tribe that surrounds them. More specifically, are the people in that person's family as well as the friends they associate with building families and creating legacies themselves. Now, some may believe that this does not matter, but think about it from this perspective, if you and the person you are dating decide to take your relationship to the next level and build a family, how beneficial would it be for your children to grow up with the children of your family and friends. From baby boomers all the way down to Millennials, most of us were fortunate enough to grow up around cousins & family friends. Growing up with a community of loved ones not only gave us someone to play with, but it also helped us develop socially, emotionally, and taught us our first lesson in loyalty towards those we love. Growing up with a tribe is pertinent to your overall growth; unfortunately, millennials have begun building families later in life, in cities and states foreign to them, with no connection to a tribe. This lack of community forces you as an adult to fend for yourself and causes your future children to develop in a setting not necessarily designed to advance social skills, such as school and after-school activities.

Future generations need to take more initiative when it pertains to building a community with family and friends. A pack should be made during early adulthood to build with one another, build together socially, community-wise, as well as economically. This way of living would allow the couples to support each other and develop a social construct for the children to thrive in and pass down to preceding generations.

# LAW 38: DON'T BLOCK YOUR BLESSING, WAITING ON MR. OR MISSES "NONEXISTENT"

The world is filled with billions of people; globally, it is comprised of many types of personalities, styles, attitudes, and so much more. I honestly believe that there is someone for each of us, and they may exist anywhere in this world. There are many who pass up the person that they should be with or the opportunity of meeting the right one, waiting on a figment of their imagination. Standards should be had by all when scouting for a significant other, but just make sure that you don't pass up the opportunity to be with the person meant for you overlooking that individual because you've set this lofty standard that may not be able to be 100% met because it truly doesn't exist. As I say, if you meet an individual with at least 70% of the things that you look for in a mate, you may want to take the time to explore the potential chance for romance. At some point in life, we all miss out on a good thing; whether it's in our explorational college years or in our early twenties, most have had the person that they should or should've been with right in front of their face but did not proceed for one reason or another. There are many reasons why individuals miss the opportunity to be with Mr. Or Misses right, but the three common reasons are that they were not mature enough to realize they met the right one. Maturity is key to understanding & becoming part of any romantic relationship. It is not unusual not to be aware that you have come across the right one, especially at an early age, when the focus is placed primarily on you and your goals. Your twenties and, for some, their early thirties are the time you spend gaining a better understanding of your own likes and dislikes; this time is also spent building yourself up mentally, spiritually, emotionally, and of course, financially. With all those things to pay attention to, it is no wonder a person could miss the opportunity to connect with an individual that could potentially be meant for them. The second common reason, is being overly career focused. Now, I will never knock anyone for placing focus on their career; in fact, I have done it myself, and it was beneficial, but it is not for everyone who chooses to do so. Some people do not know how to balance work life and personal life and, at points, become overly consumed with their career that they forget to live. Sacrificing leisure time is essential in becoming successful in this world but placing too much energy and focus one way while neglecting another focal point in your life can lead to severe social imbalances. Misallocating your time just to earn a living will hurt what you are earning your living for which is to build, build with a partner, build a family, build a life with that partner, and build a financial foundation for future children if you so choose to have any. So, remember, do not place so much emphasis on your life chasing a dollar that you place companionship, love, and family on the back burner with the potential mate especially made for you. The final reason most tend to pass up the relationship meant for them is that they feel like they may be missing something better, and this may be partially true. We all go through various stages and phases in our lives, the person you may become 5 years from now may or may not be a good fit for the partner you meet at the current phase in your life, but how can we gauge the unknown? There is no real indicator on which direction a person will grow in life; we all must use our own intuition and hope that we are making the right choice in a potential lifelong partner. Now, although we cannot tell the future, those in a relationship, especially in the dating stage, should do a 90-day audit of the person you are with. This audit will give you insight into where each person stands in the current season of their life; it will allow you to hear and see how they are preparing for their future. A relationship audit can save you from wasting time with the wrong person;

it also can reassure you that you are dating the right life partner, giving you a better outlook on a potential long-term future with that individual. No matter which reason affects you the most, just remember that a closed mind will always stop you from opening your heart.

# LAW 39: VACATIONS ARE A NECESSITY, PART WAYS WITH THE WORLD TO CONNECT WITH THE ONE YOU LOVE.

We all get caught up in the daily hustle and grind of the day. Getting up early in the morning and starting our day of work, rushing out the door, sitting in traffic, just to go to a 9 to 5, all the while forgetting to connect with our spouse or partner. Losing connection with your partner is easy to do today; with so much emphasis being placed on making money and hustle, hustle, hustle, it is easy to forget that you need time to get Intune with the person you share your time and life with. Reconnecting may be difficult to accomplish effectively while at home, especially if you have a full house or work from home. Therefore, I suggest taking a break from the day-to-day of the world and going on a vacation with your spouse. Explore domestically, explore internationally but explore together with the one you love. Vacation is not only a time to break away from work, but it is also a time to relax the spirit, mind, and body, and it is better to take this time to unwind with your partner. What makes vacation great for couples is the fact that it is a time when all stressors are set aside. During this time, you can sit with your partner and enjoy their company with little to no interruption, free from all your daily worries. Couples should take this time to have intimate conversations about interests and issues that may be on their minds. Explore new restaurants, try out new adventures while away. Take this time to say yes, instead of no, or I am not interested; keep everything within reason, of course, but explore things together that you normally wouldn't try. This display of spontaneity brings excitement to the relationship, keeping it interesting and enjoyable and giving your partner something to look forward to on the next vacation or spur-of-the-moment outing. Connecting with your loved one while in a state of peace and serenity allows both partners to express themselves with a clear mindset in a concise manner. Lack of vacations and mental breaks with your spouse can cause tension and lead to ongoing friction that will eventually affect your relationship for the long term.

# LAW 40: FIND A PERSON WHO YOU CAN INVEST IN AND INVEST WITH. A PROGRESSIVE RELATIONSHIP GIVES EACH PERSON SOMETHING TO LOOK FORWARD TO IN LIFE.

We all want to be romantically involved with someone that we can not only see us being in love with, but someone that we can see investing our all into. Time is the most valued asset that we all possess, and as explained in chapter 19, we do not have the luxury of wasting it on people who add nothing yet deplete you of everything. When finding the right one, you will know it; the connection between you and the person designed to be in your presents will transcend romance; it will incorporate time, spiritual connection, energy, and of course, economic growth. Finding a life partner is more than finding a person you love; it is also finding an individual you want to invest everything in.

Let's start with energy, connecting with an individual whose energy is in sync with yours is key. Not only does it bring balance to your life, but it also helps to shift the way you think and respond to life's daily challenges. Finding someone with positive energy helps you to not only maintain a strong bond with the individual whom you are with, but it also carries over into your work and family life as well. Someone who attracts you with positive energy will use that same energy to help add value to all aspects of your life. Next, let us discuss how to invest in a partner spiritually and how valuable that is in giving the relationship longevity. Your spiritual foundation is your base; it is the most important ground on which you stand. It is your belief system, your driving force, your overall power supply. Investing in someone spiritually means coming from the same spiritual background, imbodying the same moral compass, and displaying the same values instilled in you through your spiritual foundation. The person you are with should value speaking to a higher power through prayer or meditation. Your partner should also allow their spirituality to be the driving force of all important decision-making for themselves and for their family. Finally, let's focus on investing in someone from an economic standpoint. When investing time and energy into a person, you also want to be connected to someone with whom you would not mind building a solid financial structure. This includes being with someone you can invest with and invest in through business dealings and asset acquisition. Finding someone that you feel comfortable enough to invest in not only shows how you view them in terms of how they manage money. It also shows that you view them as a responsible person, and they are worth investing in financially for the long term. How a person oversees money with just you, will also show you how they will handle money in a complete family set up, with children and all.

# LAW 41: BOUNDARIES ARE TO BE SET, BUT TOO MANY BOUNDARIES CREATE A MAZE.

During most new relationships, most couples tend to hold back on what they like, what they are into, how they like to be dealt with, among other things. It is especially important that everyone knows exactly where everyone stands in a relationship and what the expectations are in that relationship; this is the purpose of setting boundaries. Boundaries are necessary during the dating stage and recommended during the marriage. A few boundaries that should be set within a romantic relationship is taking responsibility for your actions. We all should be taught early on in our lives about being accountable and taking responsibility for our actions, especially if the actions hurt or harm someone or something. As individuals, we need to understand the line that we should not cross; understanding this line not only helps us to avoid causing issues in the first place, but when that line is crossed, you are more aware of what was done, which will allow you to correct the issue or at least show remorse. Another boundary, and the most popular, is recognizing when a person needs space. Knowing how to read your spouse's mood & body language is vital when showing respect to an individual needing time for themselves. Most tend to forget that everyone needs a minute to sit in peace to process their thoughts. Violating that time can be deemed disrespectful and can potentially cause tension between a couple. Allow your partner to take time to themselves, whatever they do to unwind; if it's healthy, allow them. When they are ready to speak, they will open up to you. One of the final relationship boundaries I will touch on is showing respect for a person's beliefs, perspectives, differences in opinion, and feelings. We must understand and recognize that we are all individuals, and as individuals, we have our own way of viewing things that others should respect, especially our spouse. Though most relationships start with shared commonalities, our personal perspectives make us unique to others. In a relationship, it is also important to have regard for your partner's feelings; we all display emotions and harbor different feelings when it comes to certain topics & issues. To be a devoted friend and solid partner, it is important to show compassion and empathy when your spouse expresses themselves regarding different topics of discussions, especially ones of a sensitive nature. Knowing your spouse's boundaries not only shows you care but also displays a great deal of respect for the individual and allows them to see that you carry an important level of regard for their feelings & wellbeing.

# LAW 42: GOD WILL SEND YOU A SPOUSE, BUT GOD HELPS THOSE WHO HELP THEMSELVES, SO MEET YOUR FUTURE PARTNER HALFWAY.

To meet the future love of your life, it takes effort and preparation; nothing good comes your way by chance; the right thing tends to present itself to you when you least expect it, yet fully are prepared to receive it. The single life can be tough, especially when you are actively searching for love, but you must stay the course; otherwise, you will never be able to find the person you are meant to be with. Searching for a mate takes effort, an effort that most have gotten away from, out the convivence of dating apps and social media. Not to place full blame on these tools, but they have assisted in the lack of social interaction among people in society today. Once upon a time, most people would meet at social gatherings, congregating together, getting to know each other, connecting with those with who you share things in common with. Now, social interactions are done primarily through the dm or tweets. It has made people feel that all they need to do sit at home and their dream man or woman will show up on their doorstep like an Amazon prime next-day package. To come across the right one, you must put your feet to the pavement and get out into the world so that you can feel the energy of your potential mate. Depending on what you are looking for will determine the environment you should be in. For instance, you would not look up for a wholesome mild manner man or woman in the VIP section of a nightclub; you also wouldn't find a fitness model at a hot dog eating contest. Put yourself in the environment of your desired mate, and make sure you are prepared mentally, emotionally, and financially to receive the person you desire when in the vicinity of said person. Making yourself accessible but not overly accessible is necessary if you plan on truly finding someone who is evenly yoked for you. Putting out minimal to no effort while constantly staying in your own bubble will leave you aged and alone. Remember, if you put no effort into finding the right mate, what makes you think you'd suddenly put any effort into keeping them? You only play how you practice.

# LAW 43: DON'T CHASE WHAT YOU ARE NOT PREPARED TO CATCH.

Everyone thinks that they want a gorgeous-looking man or woman, who is driven, goal-oriented, with everything going for themselves, until they get that man or woman and realize they are not mentally capable of dealing with a desirable individual. It is easy to fantasize about a beautiful man or woman while looking at them on a YouTube video or scrolling through your social media timeline liking their photos, but what happens when you really have a shot at dating one of the people you spend time fawning over, are you prepared? Are you mentally prepared to deal with all that comes with dating a nice-looking person who has an amazing career and their head on straight? There is a lot that comes with dating a well-put-together overachiever with grand expectations. Whether the person has grown up always expecting the most out of life or figured it out for themselves as they became more well-rounded, someone of a certain caliber will always want to do, see, achieve, and experience the most that life has to offer. This may be tough for someone who lacks the same drive and intensity as the person they desire to be with. An overachieving man or woman will settle for nothing less than what they have worked hard to attain. Though a person searching for that type of person believes that is what they need in their life to propel them forward; they must be mentally prepared to receive the push that would come from that driven individual. No one's goal in a romantic relationship, or any relationship for that matter, should be to be a hindrance. Being romantically involved with a partner that strives to thrive and not just exist in the world, and you, not complimenting what they are working for, will be nothing more than a burden, if anything at all.

Looks are important to a great deal of people looking for a better half, but it needs to be understood that dealing with someone who is a go-getter and visually appealing to most comes with some level of responsibility. It is easy to say what you would like to have look wise if you've never had it, mainly because you do not know what all can accompany that great-looking person you are pursuing. When dealing with someone who is all around desirable, it takes a secure individual with the self-awareness and confidence to be able to handle that person and the attention they will garner. Twenty years ago, all a person had to worry about was someone working to gain the attention of their significant other by approaching them in the street or flirting with their partner in a social environment. Today, a person has to factor in the wild world of social media and the many platforms that Billions occupy. Dm's, post comments, YouTube video chat comments, random photos, displaying anything and everything, even things that may be looked at as offensive. These are all things that must be considered when dating today, especially when you are dating or pursuing an individual that is considered a hot commodity. In spite of all the things written, if you feel that you can deal with the person that "has it all", then go for it, go for it with confidence and vigor, allow that person of your dreams to motivate you to become all you hope to be in life. Allow your dream man or woman to drive you to be the best version of yourself, thus pushing them to go even harder on their goals. Never shortchange yourself, go for what you want, just make sure to have your mind prepared, and you should have no trouble maintaining a quality relationship with the person that attracted you in every way.

# LAW 44: WITH NO FOUNDATION, YOUR RELATIONSHIP WILL CRUMBLE.

A relationship is not based on the length of time you spend together; it's based on the foundation you've built together. The foundation of a romantic relationship is what will drive it to the very end, so what should that foundation consist of? First and foremost, your spirituality should be the basis of any loving relationship because it is based around God and the love of God. When entering a relationship as an adult, the end goal should be marriage, regardless of if you are 21 or 51; if the end game is not marriage, then ultimately, it is a relationship with no purpose and no base to build up from. Spiritual foundation should be the basis for all strong, meaningful relationships; it is what connects two individuals to one another. Having a spiritual foundation creates allies out of you and your partner, specifically towards growing and evolving in all aspects of life. No romantic relationship can have success without it being a three-way relationship between you, your significant other, and God as the nucleus. That spiritual base creates a feeling of freedom, freedom amongst the couple that can be their authentic selves around each other no matter what. A strong spiritual foundation strengthens respect and compassion within the relationship, allowing each person to be unapologetically flawed without judgement. The core values of the relationship will primarily be based on the couple's spiritual connection; those beliefs will dictate your behavior and personal perspectives on how to navigate and live life. As you can see, the base on which you build your relationship on is important; though the topic of spirituality is not something that most people discuss immediately, it should be because there is no need in putting energy into something that will never have the legs to stand the test of time.

# FINAL THOUGHTS

If you made it to this part of the reading, then you truly are serious about your relationship journey. Not only have you taken the first step in figuring out yourself, but also figuring out your partner or future spouse. Relationships can be tough on all fronts, but those who tend to succeed the most are those who are willing to put time, energy, and effort into building the strongest foundation possible. Being single is not a crime, but we all need one another to truly bring the best out of each other. I wish you all immense success in your relationship journey, remember follow your heart, & keep God involved in all your affairs and longevity will follow you in your relationship for a lifetime.

# ABOUT THE AUTHOR

Some of the best examples in our lives come from those standing right next to us, and no words could be any truer than when it pertains to author Robert Minor. Growing up in a three-bedroom home with thirteen other relatives, Robert learned how love could get you through the toughest of times. Robert was fortunate to grow up in a loving family with love all around him, but no greater example of love was displayed than the love he saw from his grandmother and grandfather, who has been married for close to 65 years, as well as the 17-year marriage of his mother and late father Robert Senior. These examples displayed by his loved ones not only set the standard, but also gave Robert the desire to only attach himself to love that is real and assist others in doing the same. Next to a solid spiritual foundation, the right partner is the next building block in building a strong family structure, something recognized by Robert even before his teenage years. Now on his own personal journey, Robert hopes to past down lessons learned & practices implemented in his own personal relationships that has allowed growth and the attraction of new blessings to enter his life. As he always states,

"We need each other, rather we believe so or not, the faster we believe in that fact the better off we'll be for the future and beyond."